Text Copyright © Xist Publishing 2023
Illustration Copyright © Brenda Ponnay 2023
First Edition
All Rights Reserved.
No portion of this book may be reproduced without express permission from the publisher.

Published proudly in the State of Texas, USA by Xist Publishing
www.xistpublishing.com
24200 Southwest Freeway Suite 402- 290 Rosenberg, TX 77471

eISBN: 978-1-5324-4358-9
Perfect Bound ISBN: 978-1-5324-4360-2
Hardcover ISBN: 978-1-5324-4359-6

Why Was Six Afraid of Seven?
{Illustrated Math Jokes for Kids}

Stephanie Rodriguez   Brenda Ponnay

Why was the math book sad?

Three paper bags contain a total of 59 apples. The first and second bags contain a total of 11 apples. The second and third bags contain a total of 18 apples. How many apples are in the first and third bags together?

A right triangle has one non-hypotenuse side length of 3 inches and the hypotenuse measures 5 inches. What is the length of the other non-hypotenuse side?

Ten people order pizza. If each person gets 2 slices and each pizza has 4 slices, how many pizzas should they order?

What is the surface area of a cube that has a width of 2cm, height of 2 cm and length of 2 cm?

A vending machine accepts only nickels and dimes. A bag of chips cost 85 cents. Owen has 4 dimes and enough nickels to get the bag of chips. How many nickels does Owen have?

Because it had too many problems.

What did the triangle say to the circle?

You're pointless.

Why didn't the two 4's want any dinner?

Because they already 8.

What do you get when you divide the circumference of a Jack-o-lantern by its diameter?

Pumpkin Pi!

What did one math book say to the other?

Don't ask me. I've got my own problems.

What do you call a number that won't stay still?

A roamin' numeral.

What did zero say to the number eight?

Nice belt.

What do mathematicians do after it snows?

Make snow angles.

What is a math teacher's favorite sum?

Summer!

What do a dollar and the moon have in common?

They both have four quarters.

Why couldn't Pi get a driver's license?

415926535 8979323846 2643383279 5028841971 6939937510 5820974

It didn't know when to stop.

What's a mathematician's favorite animal?

A pi-thon.

Why does algebra make you a better dancer?

Because you learn the algo-rhythmn.

What did one decimal say to the other?

Did you get my point?

What's a bird's favorite kind of math?

Owl-gebra.

What's the best way to find a math tutor?

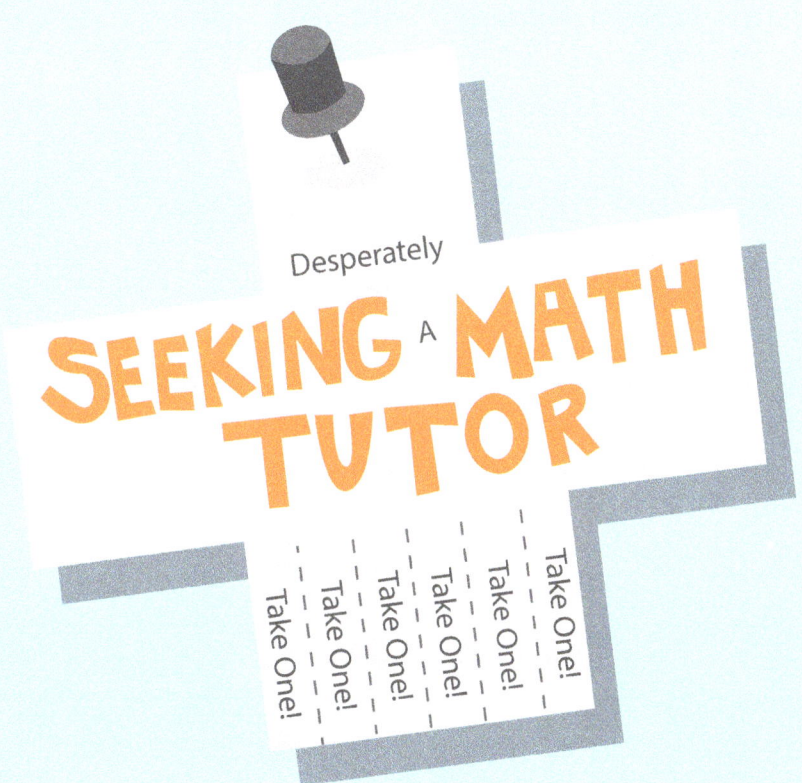

Place an add.

If you had 8 apples in one hand and 5 apples in the other, what would you have?

Really big hands.

What is the most mathematical insect?

The arithme-tick.

www.ingramcontent.com/pod-product-compliance
Lightning Source LLC
LaVergne TN
LVHW070949070426
835507LV00030B/3473